Handwriting

Workbook 1
Patterns

Rachel Davis MBE
and Manreet Ratan

Unit 1: Practising patterns

Draw over and copy the lines.

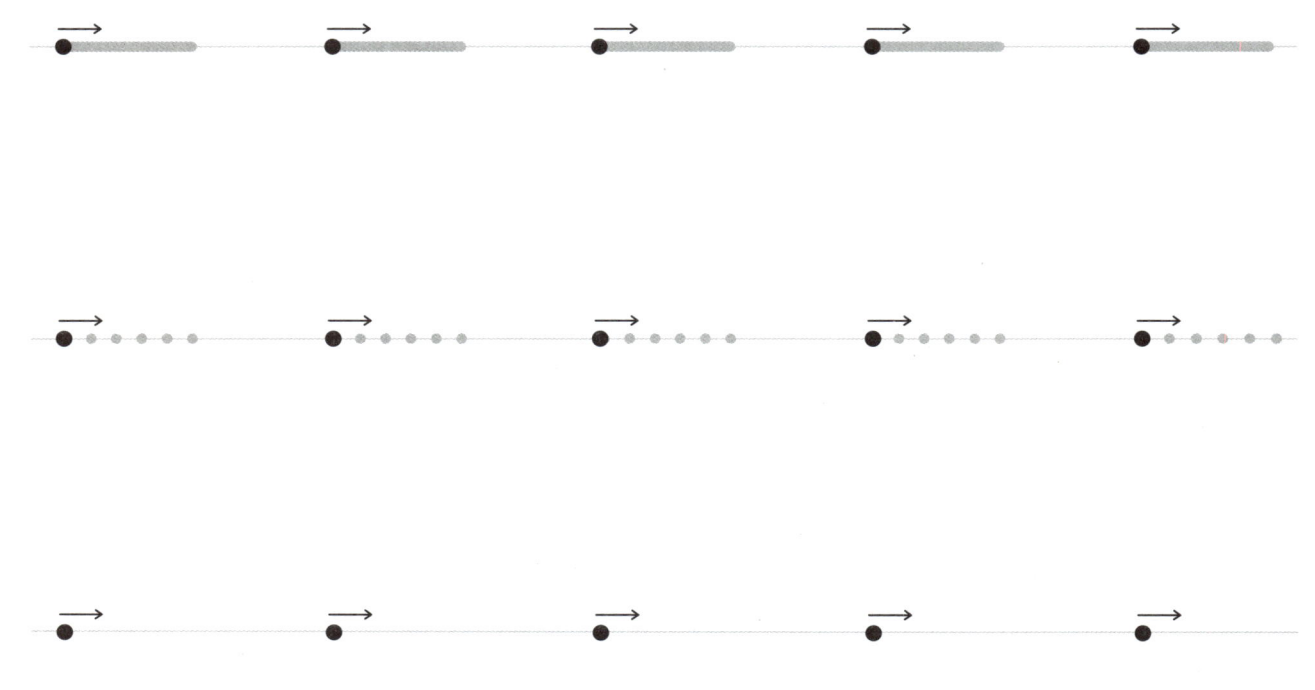

Draw over and copy the lines.

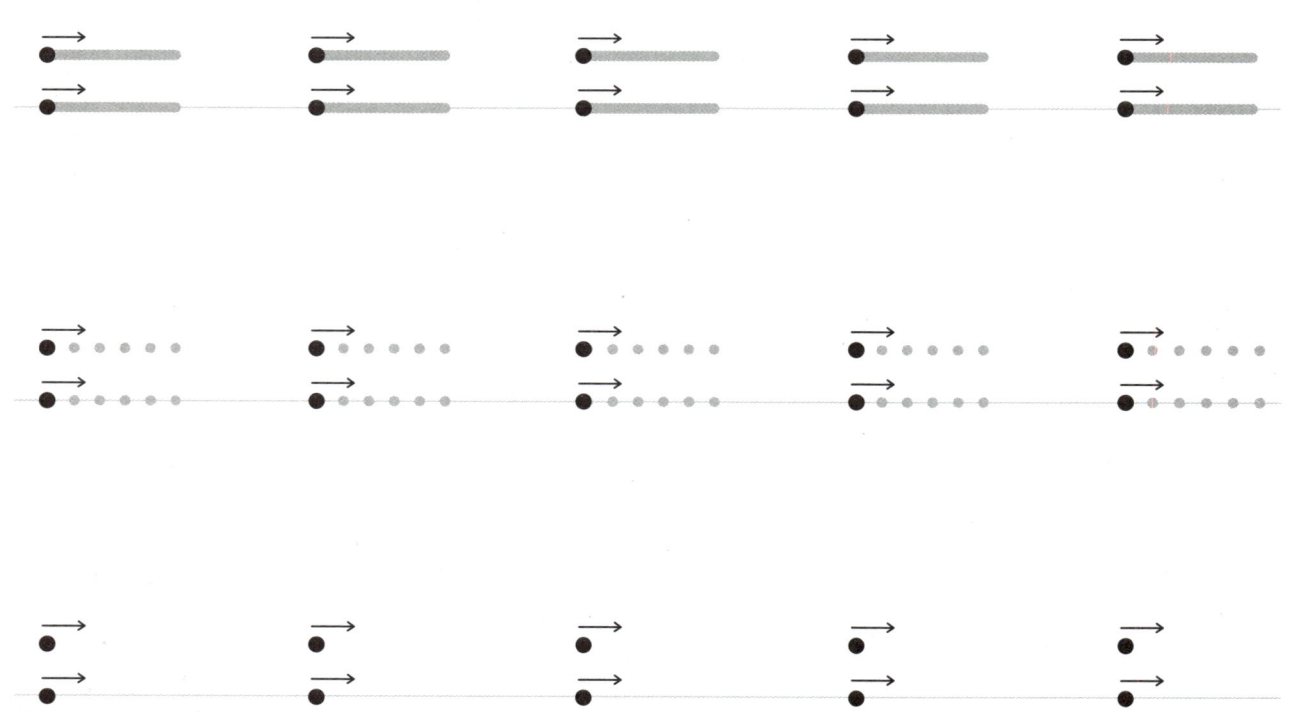

Unit 1: Practising patterns

Unit 1: Practising patterns

Draw over and copy the lines.

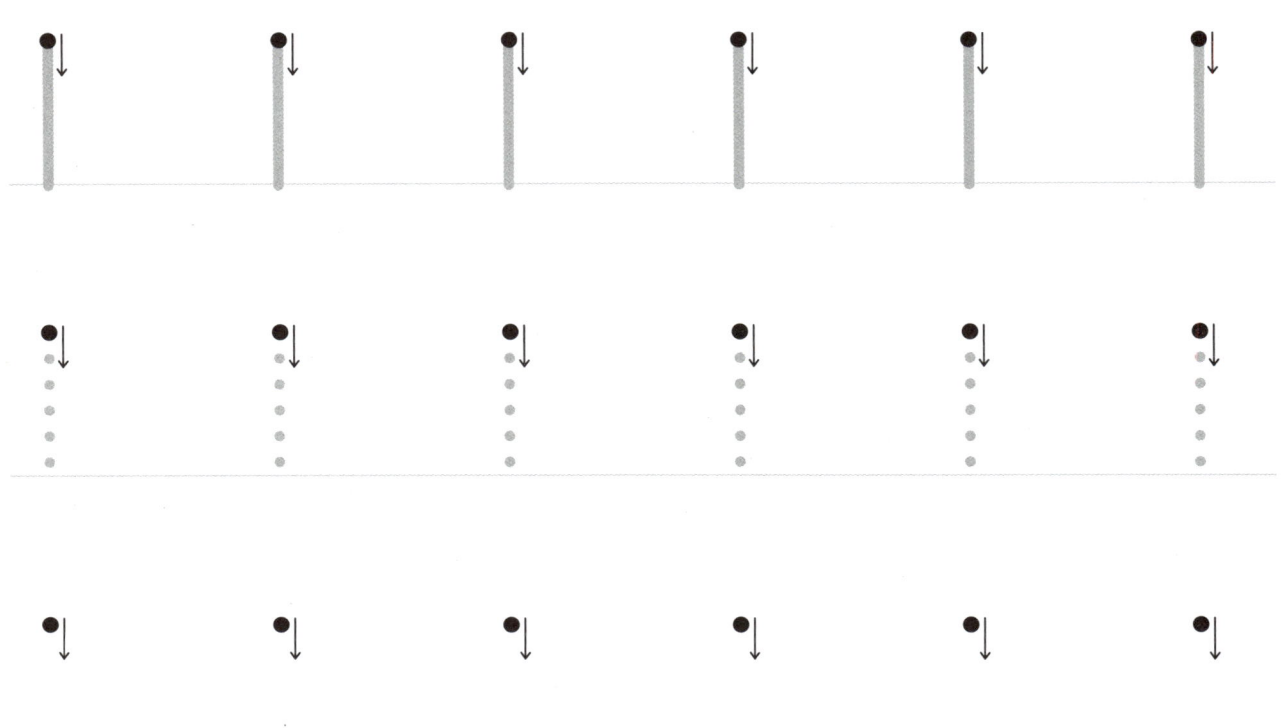

Draw over and copy the lines.

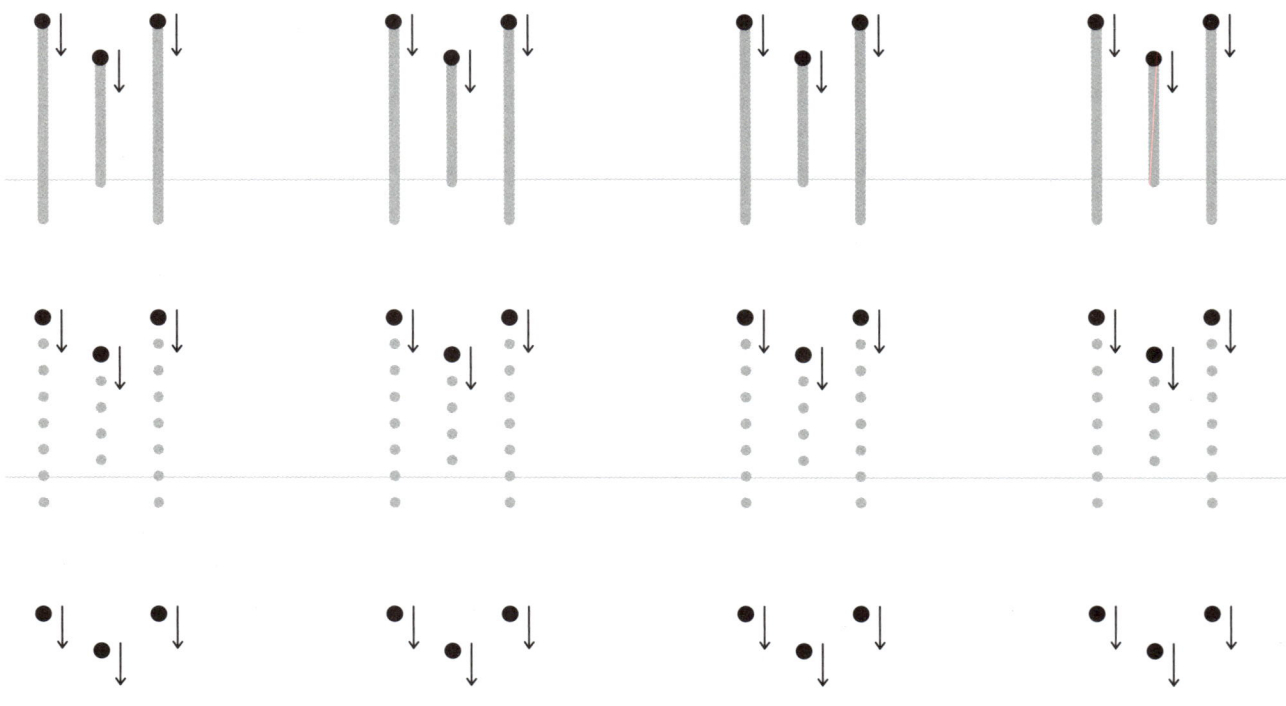

Unit 1: Practising patterns

Practice picture

Draw the rain drops.

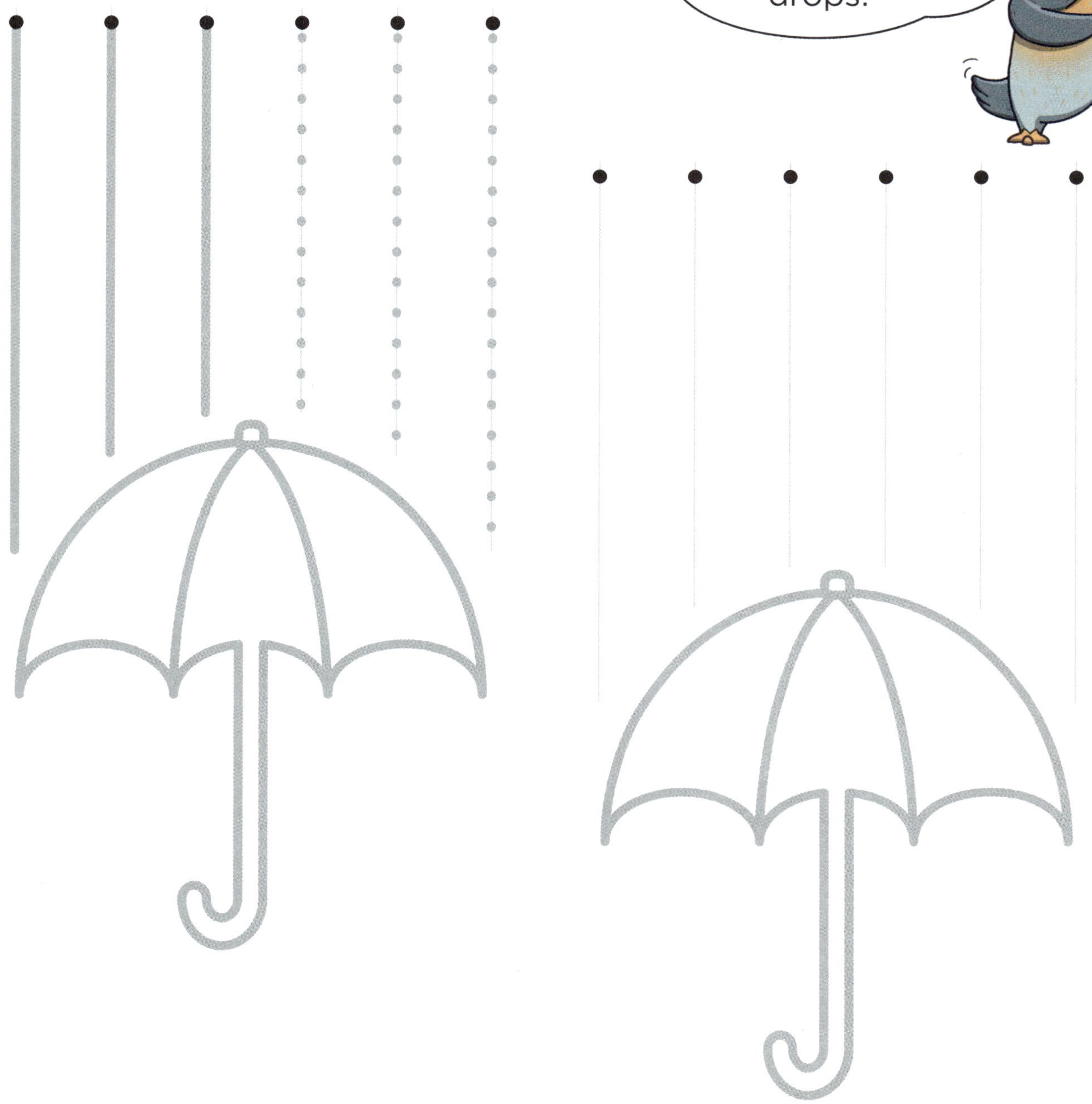

Pattern check-up

Unit 1: Practising patterns

Draw over and copy the wavy lines.

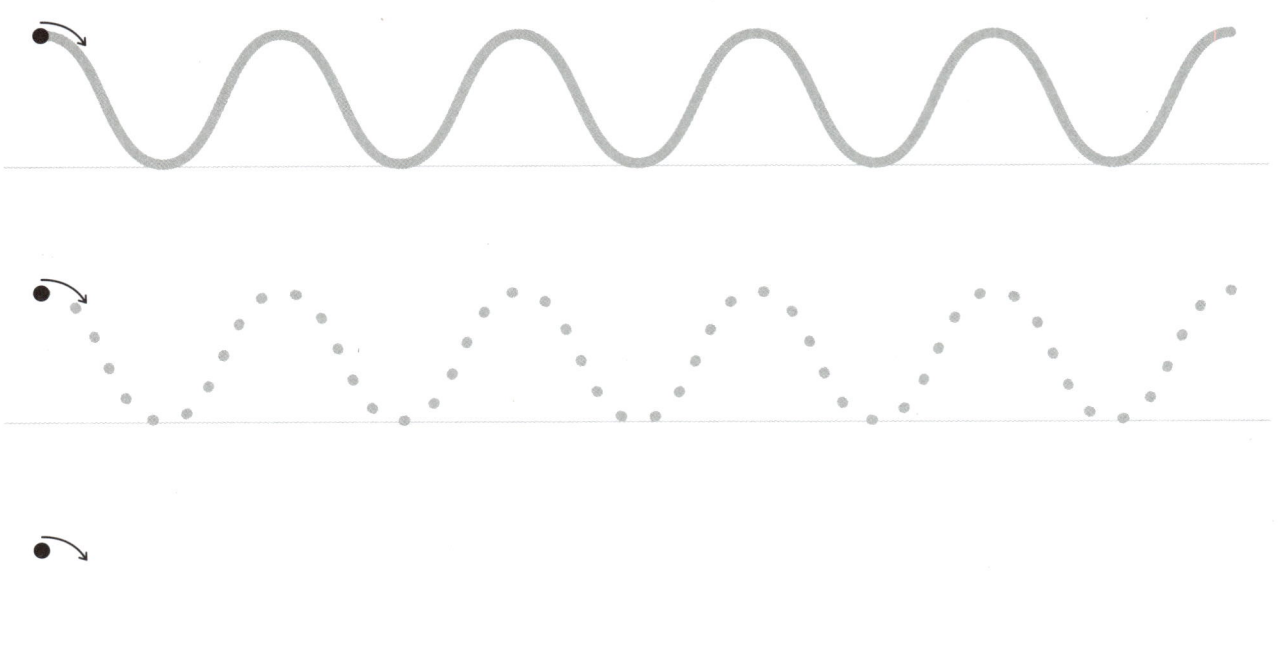

Draw over and copy the wavy lines.

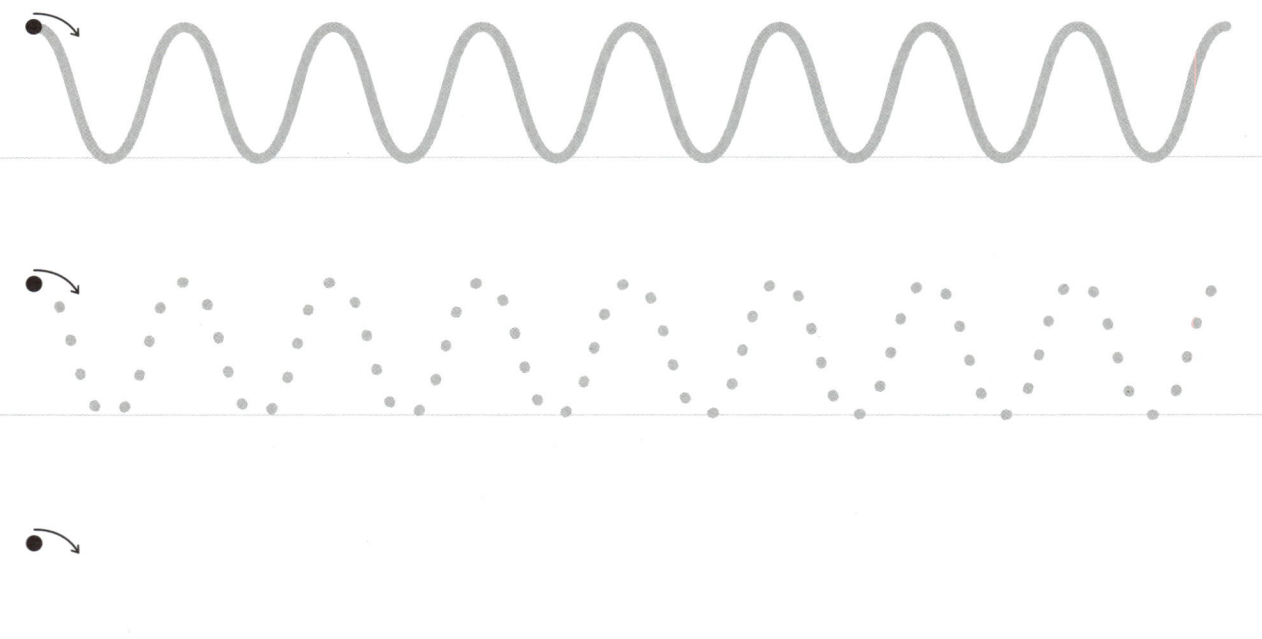

Unit 1: Practising patterns

Practice picture

Draw waves under the boat.

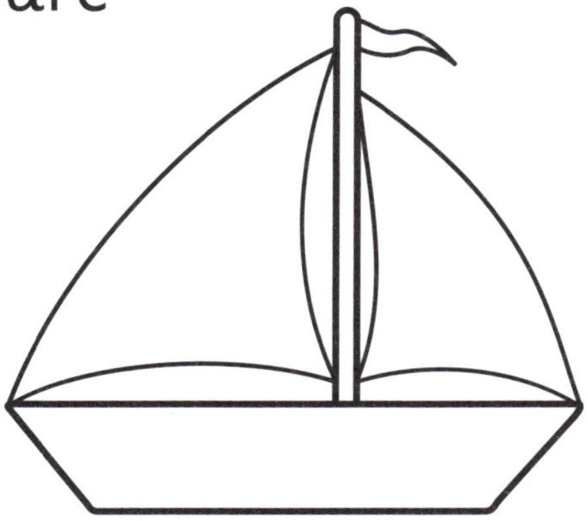

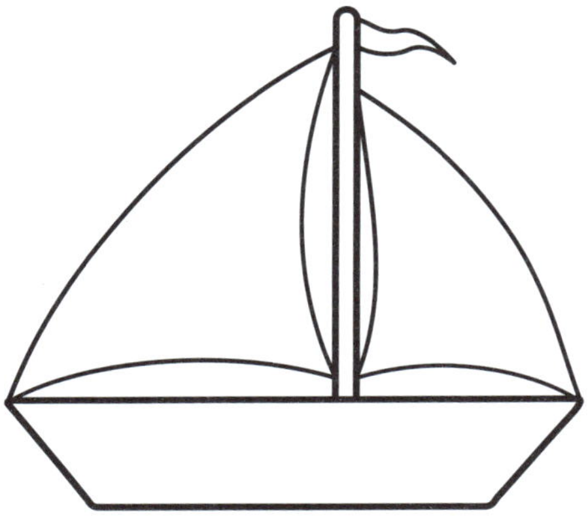

Pattern check-up

Unit 1: Practising patterns

Draw over and copy the circles.

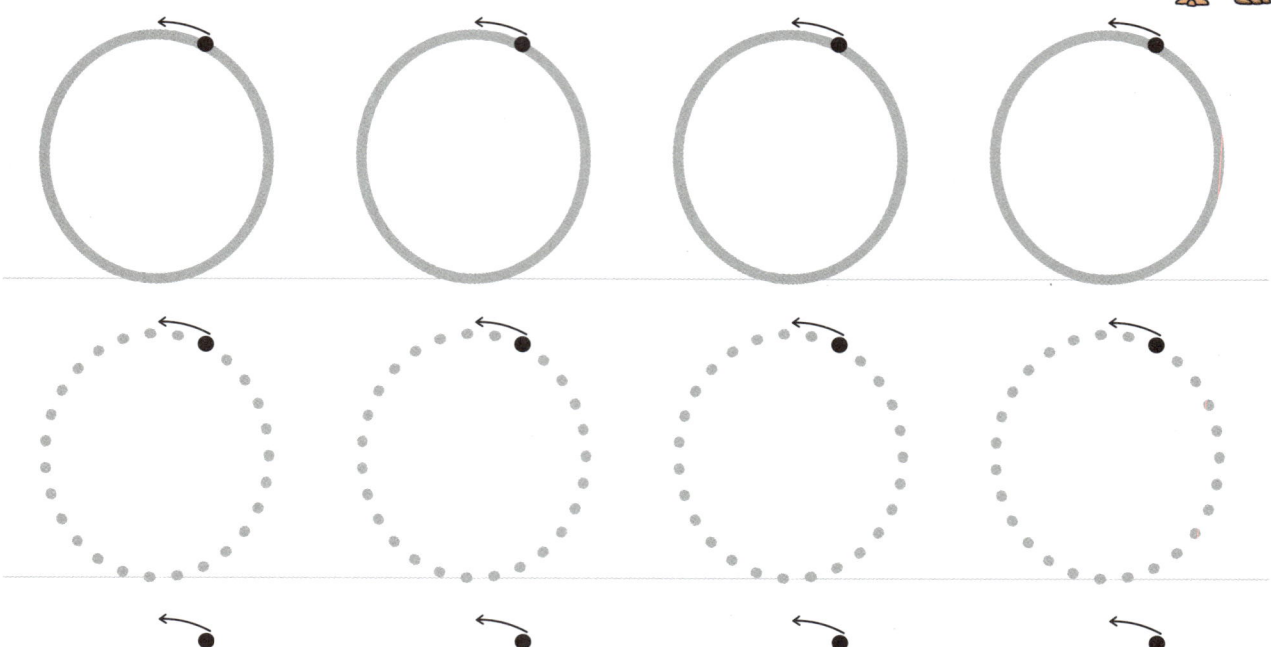

Draw over and copy the circles.

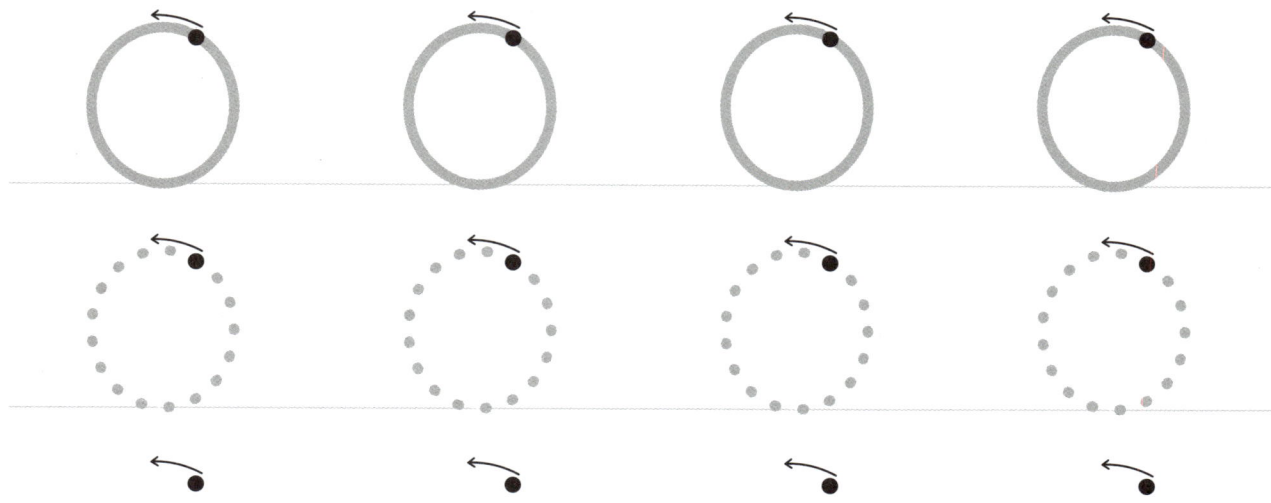

Unit 1: Practising patterns

Practice picture

Draw the circles on the octopus.

Pattern check-up

Unit 1: Practising patterns

Draw over and copy the curves.

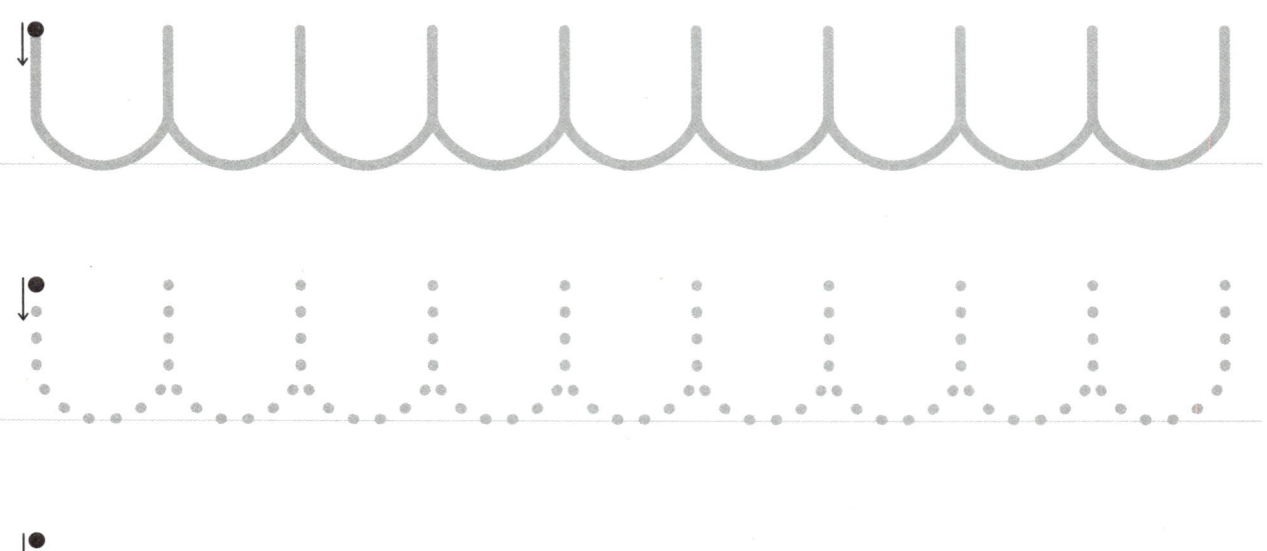

Draw over and copy the curves.

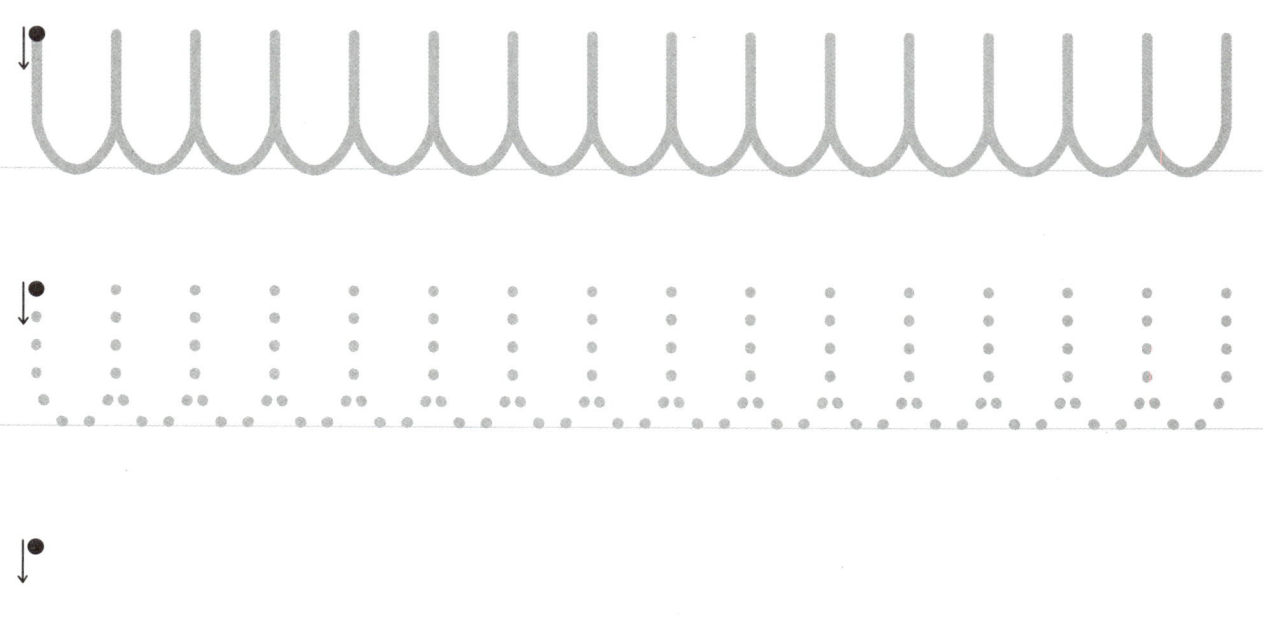

Unit 1: Practising patterns

Practice picture

Draw the curves on the cup.

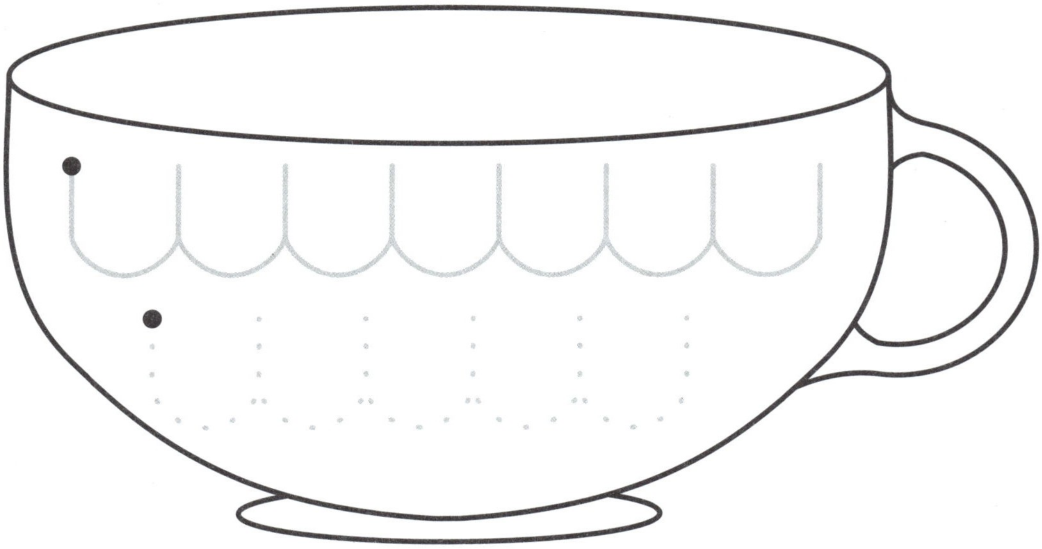

Pattern check-up

Unit 1: Practising patterns

Draw over and copy the curves.

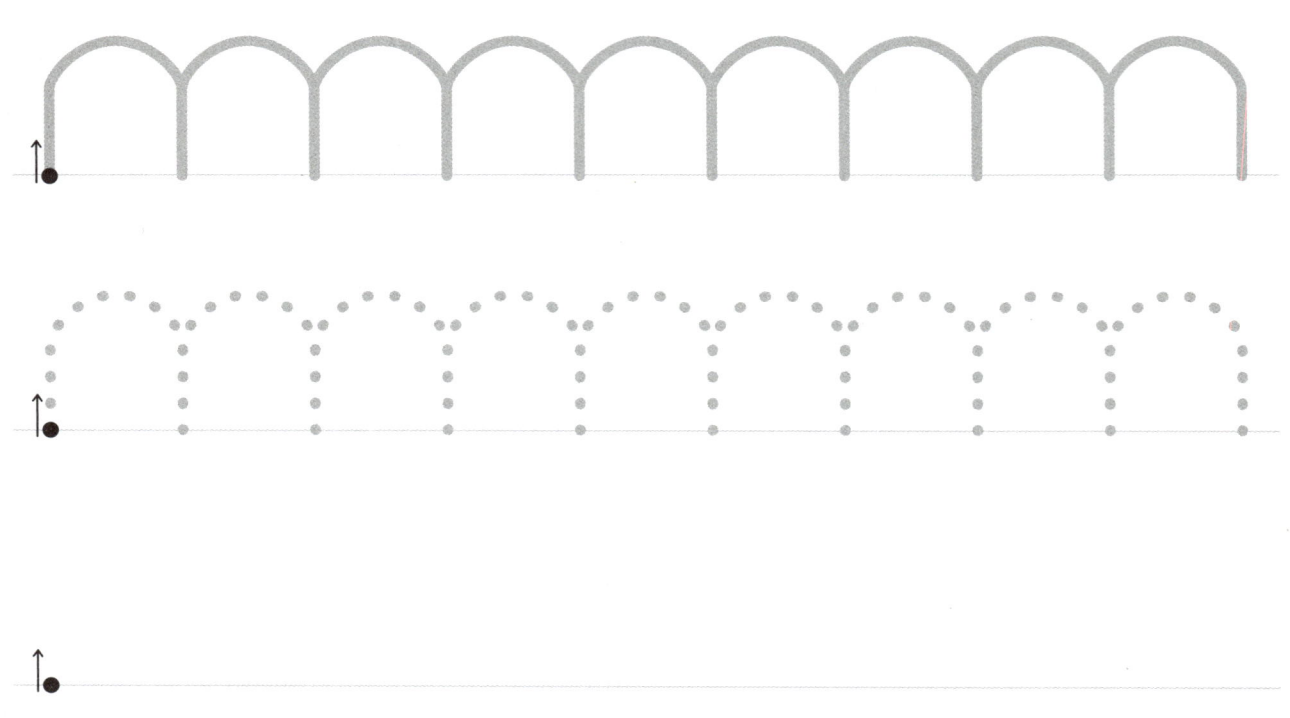

Draw over and copy the curves.

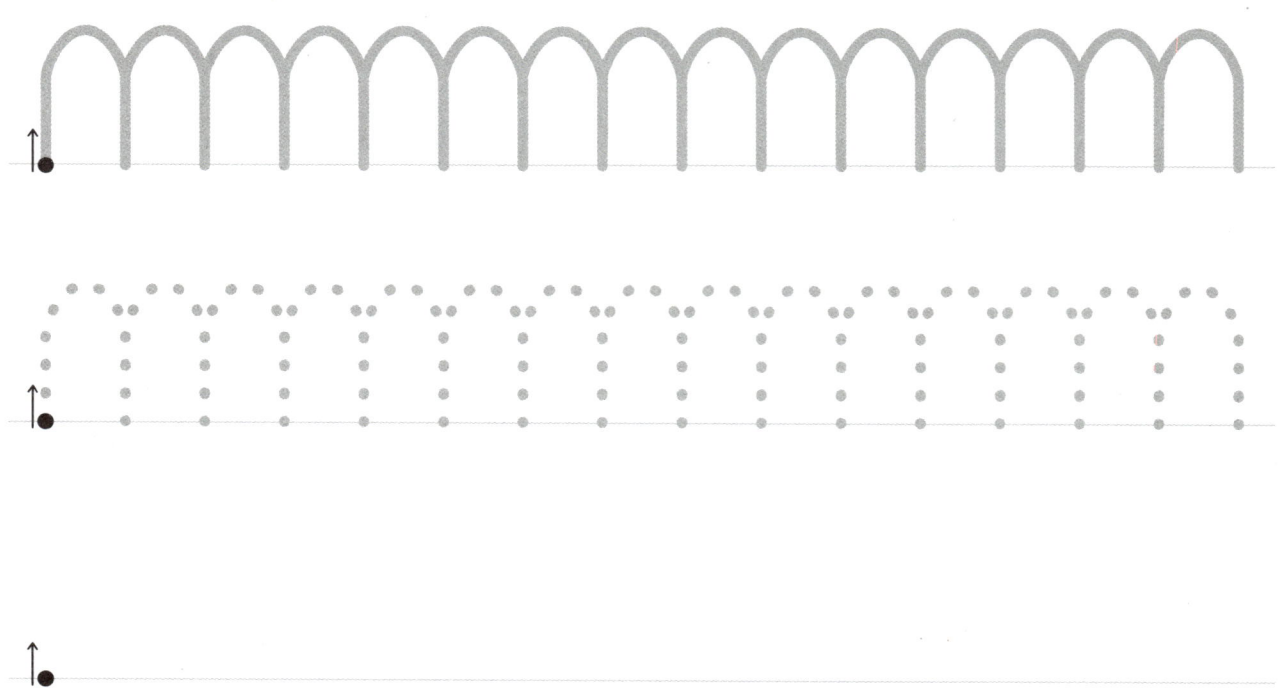

Unit 1: Practising patterns

Practice picture

Draw the curves on the sock.

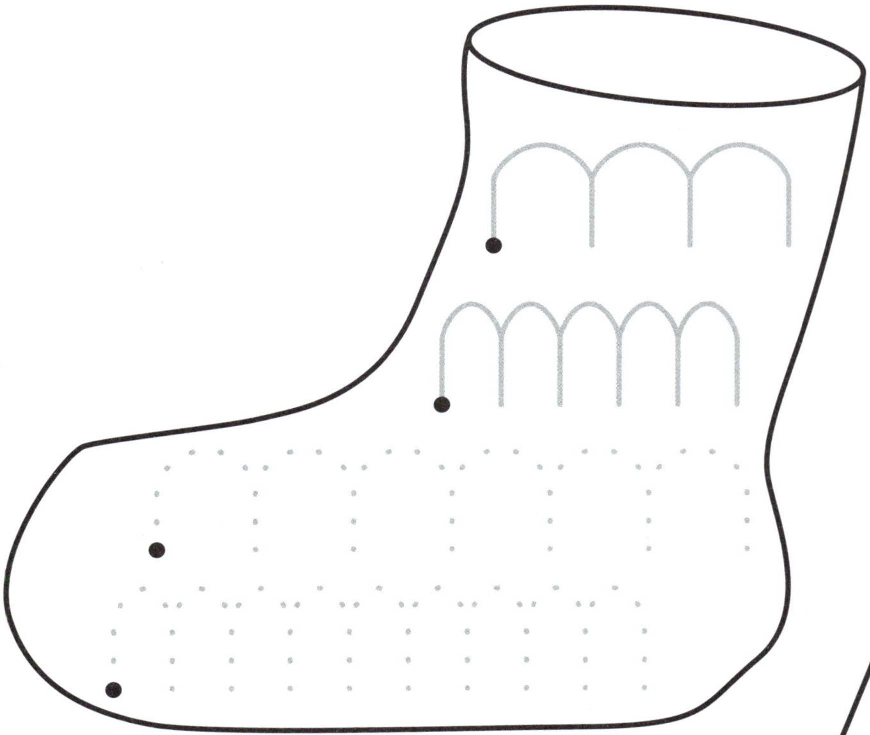

Pattern check-up

Unit 1: Practising patterns

Draw over and copy the curves.

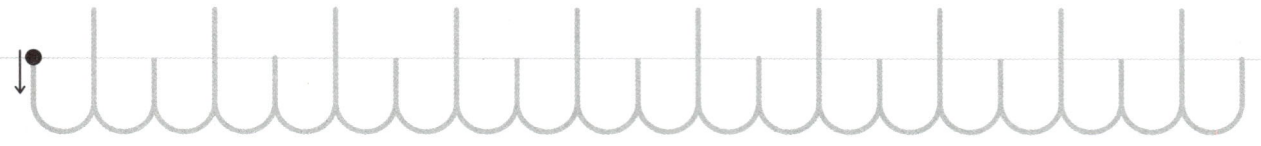

Draw over and copy the curves.

Unit 1: Practising patterns

Practice picture

Draw the curves on the rug.

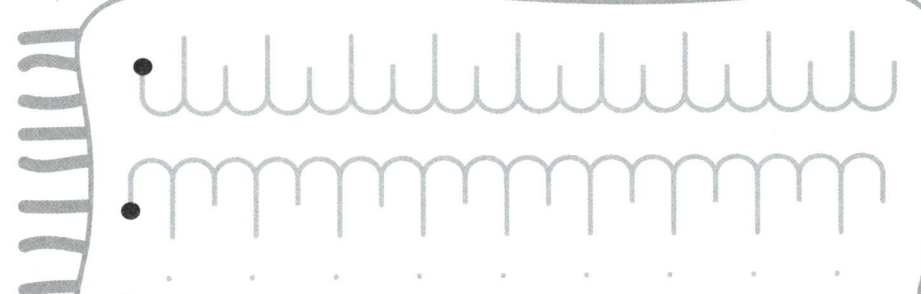

Pattern check-up

Unit 1: Practising patterns

Draw over and copy the curves.

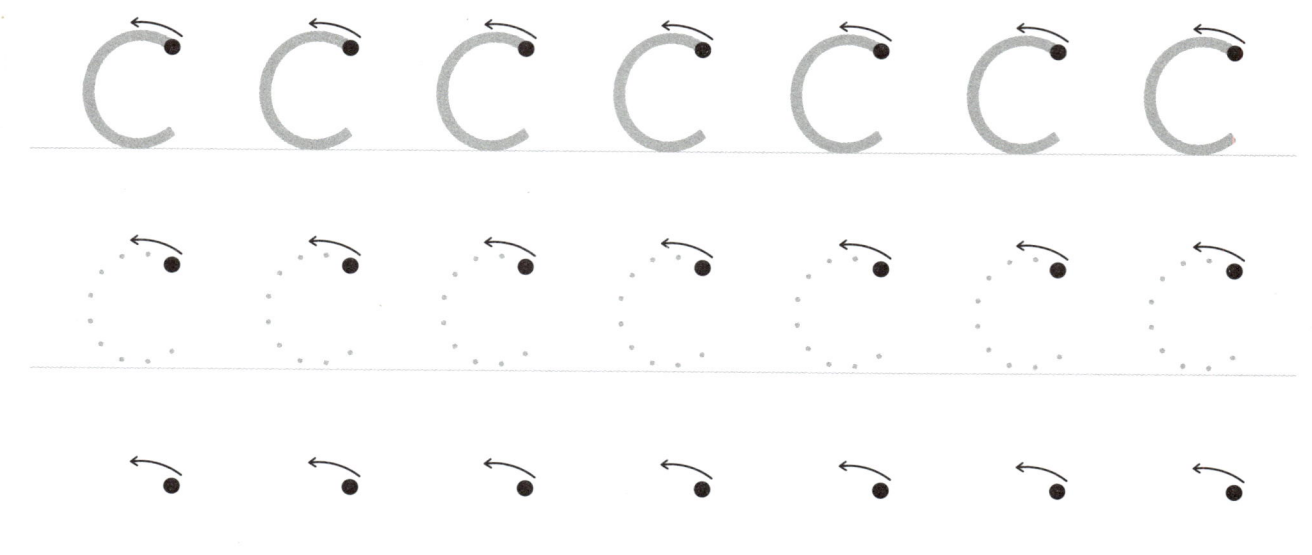

Draw over and copy the curves.

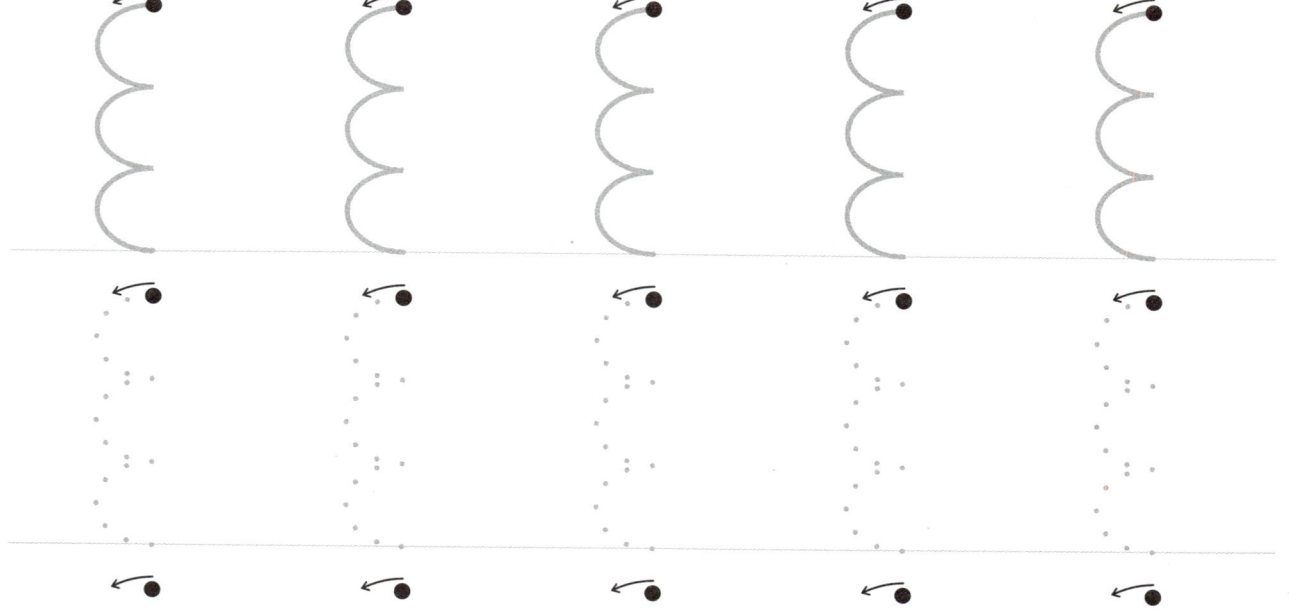

Unit 1: Practising patterns

Practice picture

Draw the curves on the balloon.

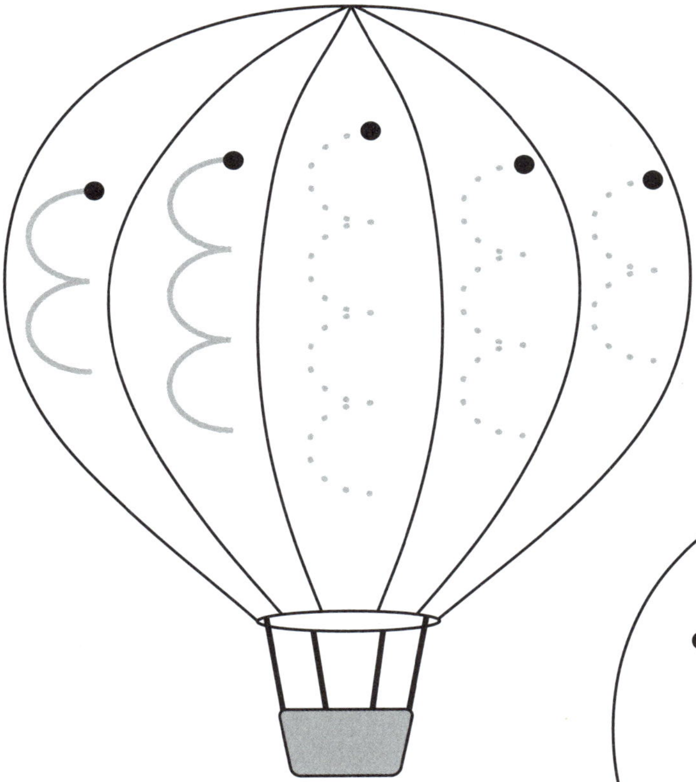

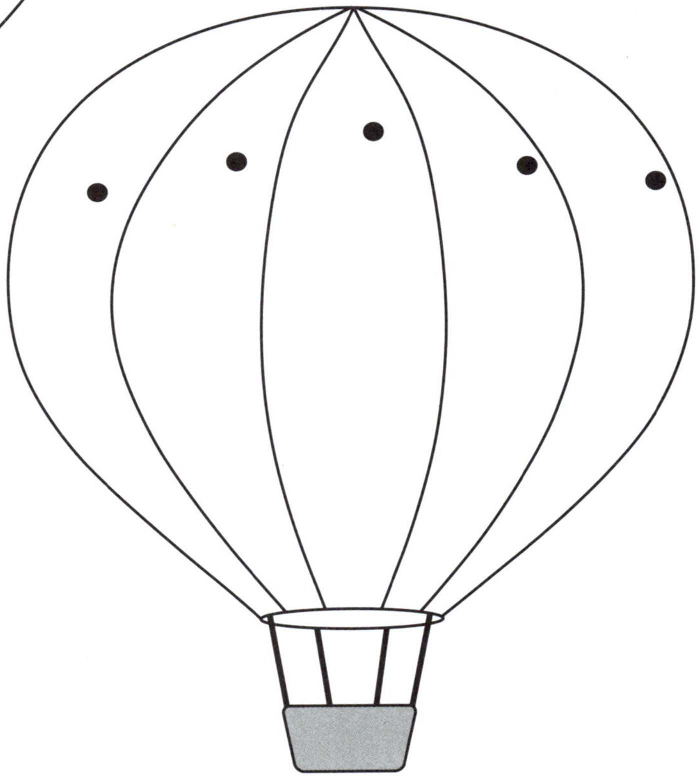

Pattern check-up

Unit 1: Practising patterns

Draw over and copy the spirals.

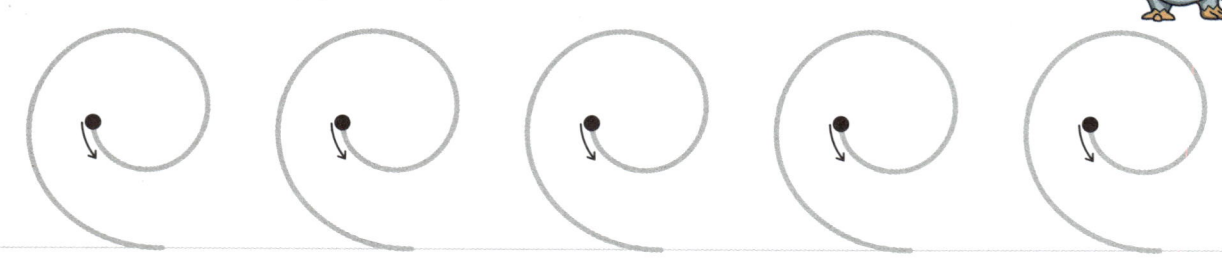

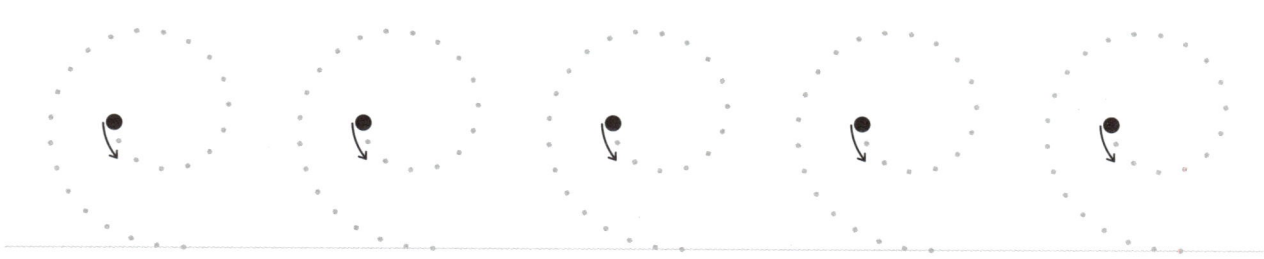

Draw over and copy the spirals.

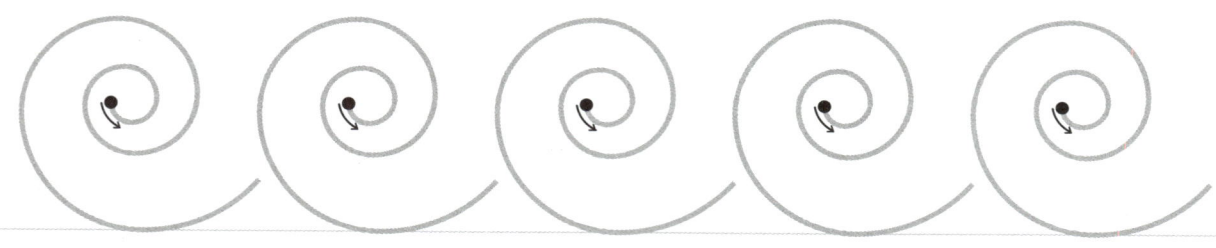

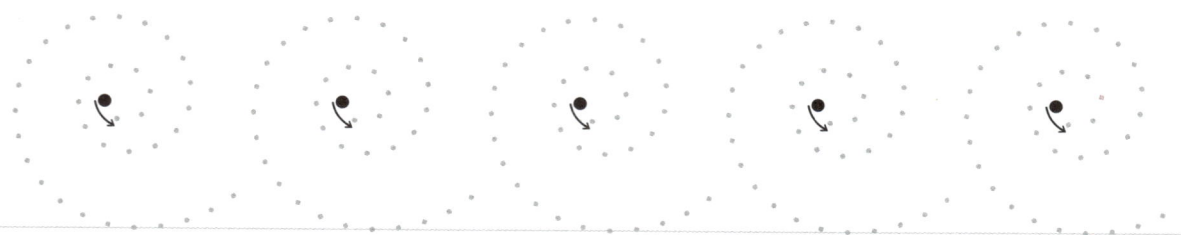

Unit 1: Practising patterns

Practice picture

"Draw the spirals. Keep your pencil on the page."

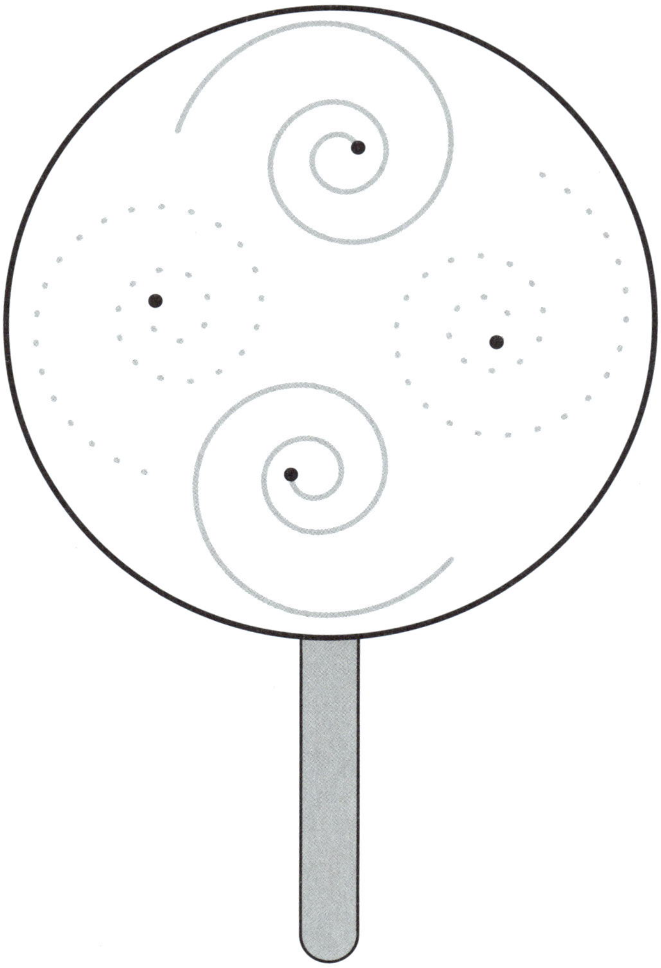

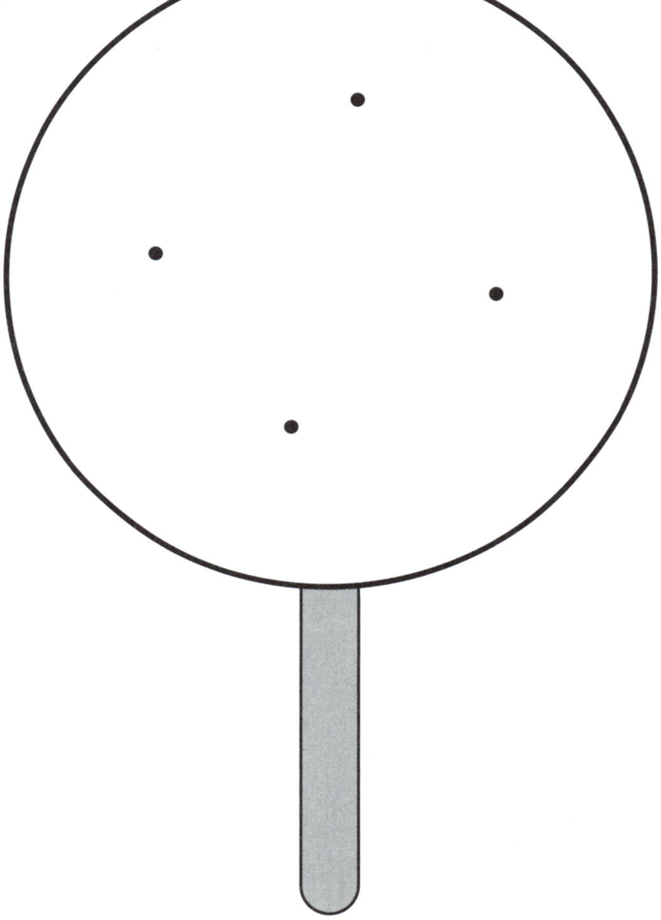

Pattern check-up

Unit 1: Practising patterns

Draw over and copy the crosses.

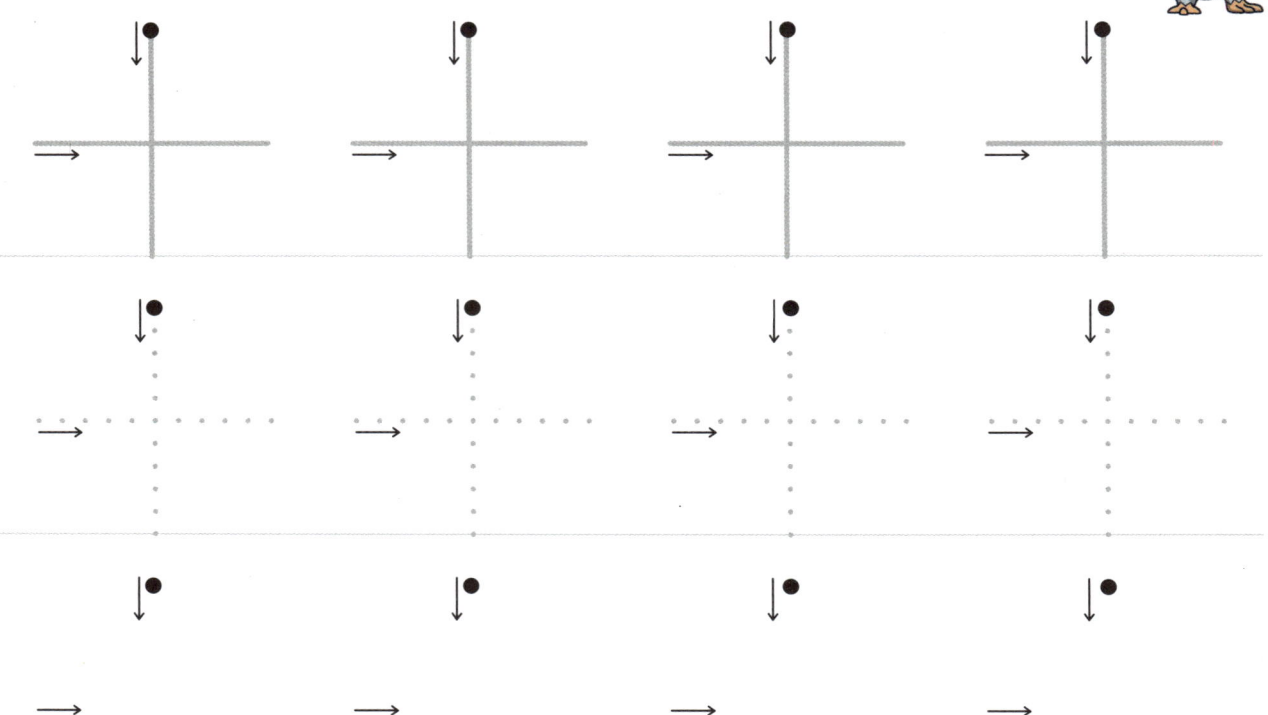

Draw over and copy the crosses.

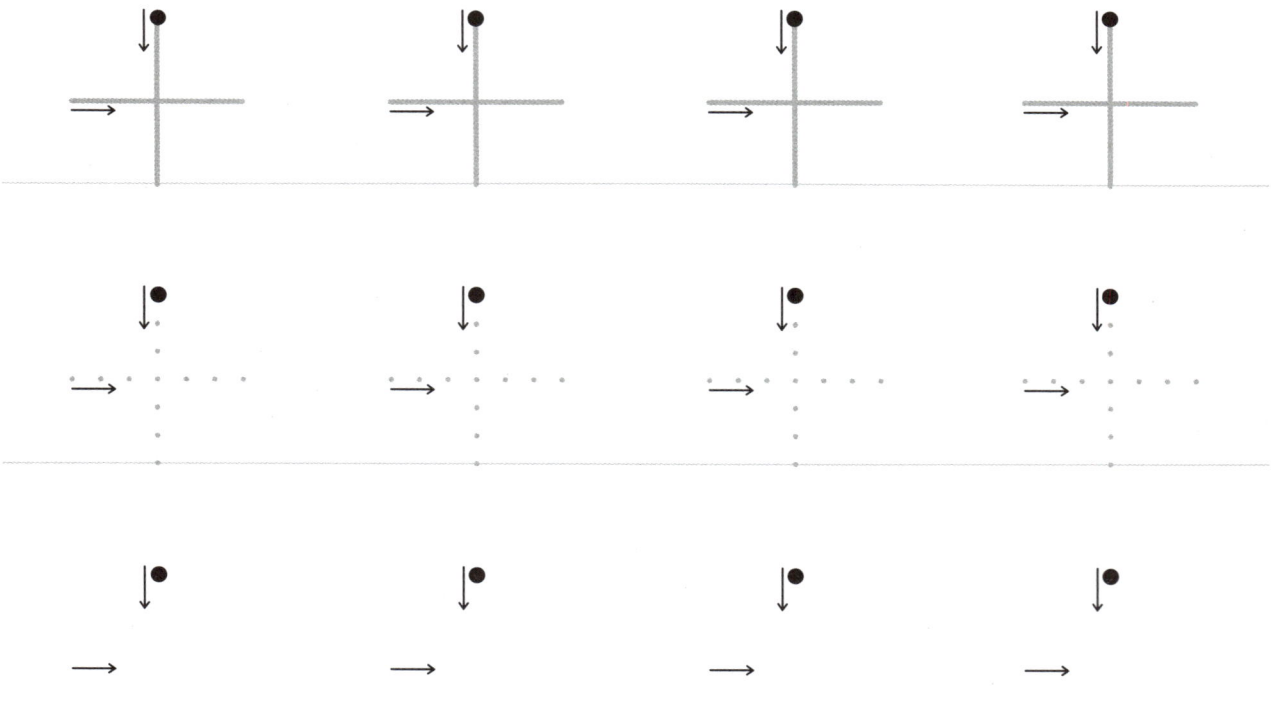

Unit 1: Practising patterns

Draw over and copy the turrets.

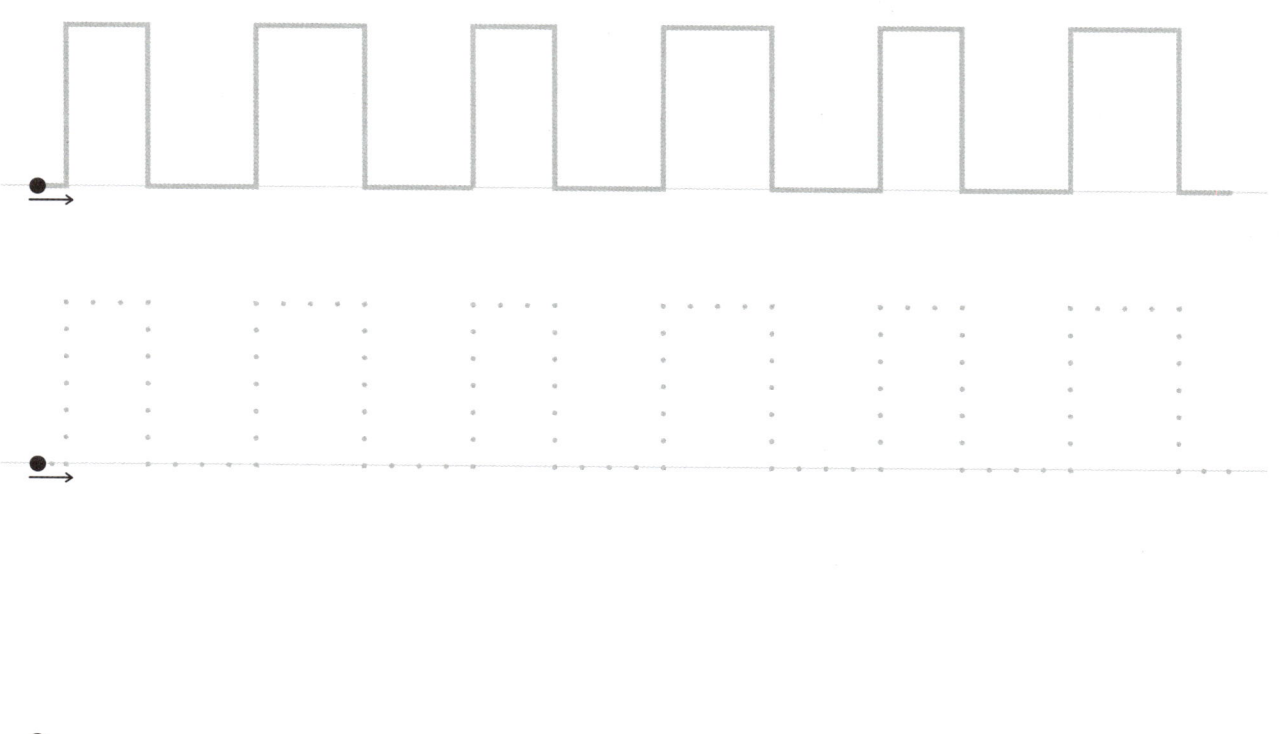

Draw over and copy the turrets.

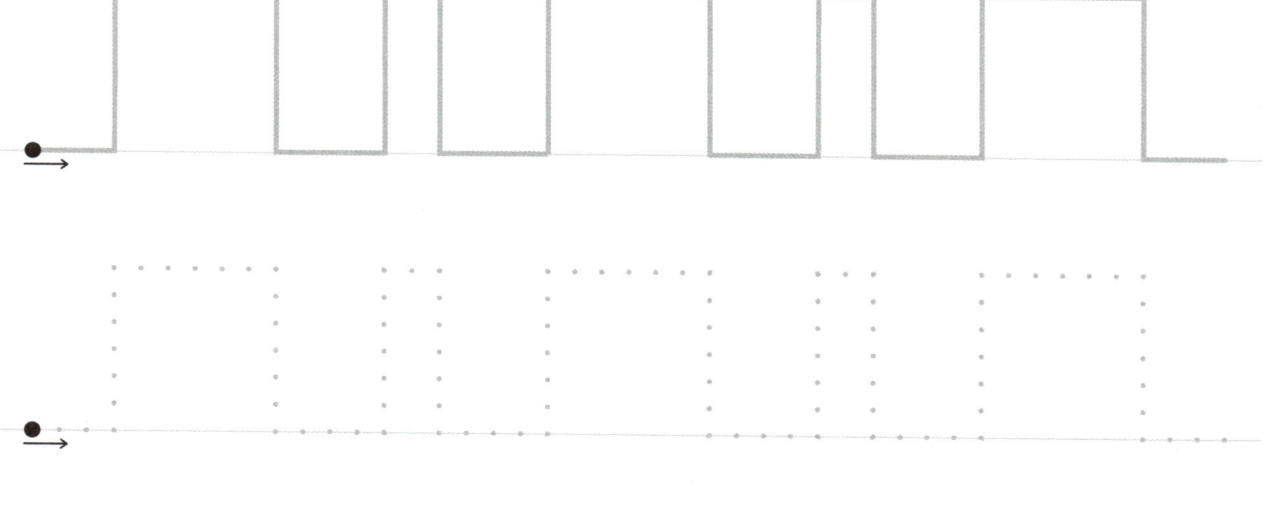

Unit 1: Practising patterns

Practice picture

Draw the turrets on the castle.

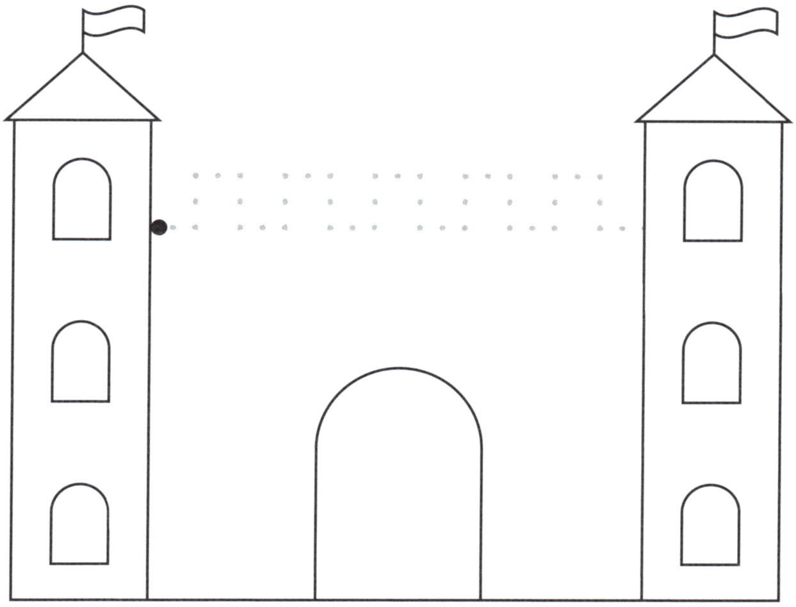

Pattern check-up

Unit 1: Practising patterns

Draw over and copy the lines.

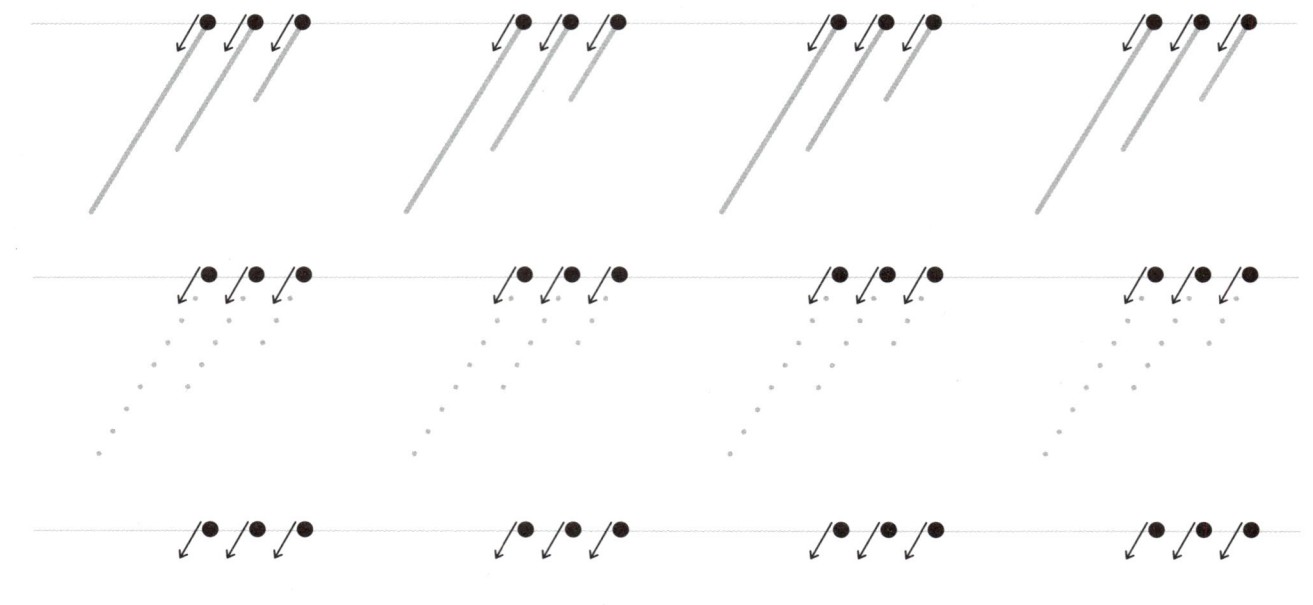

Draw over and copy the lines.

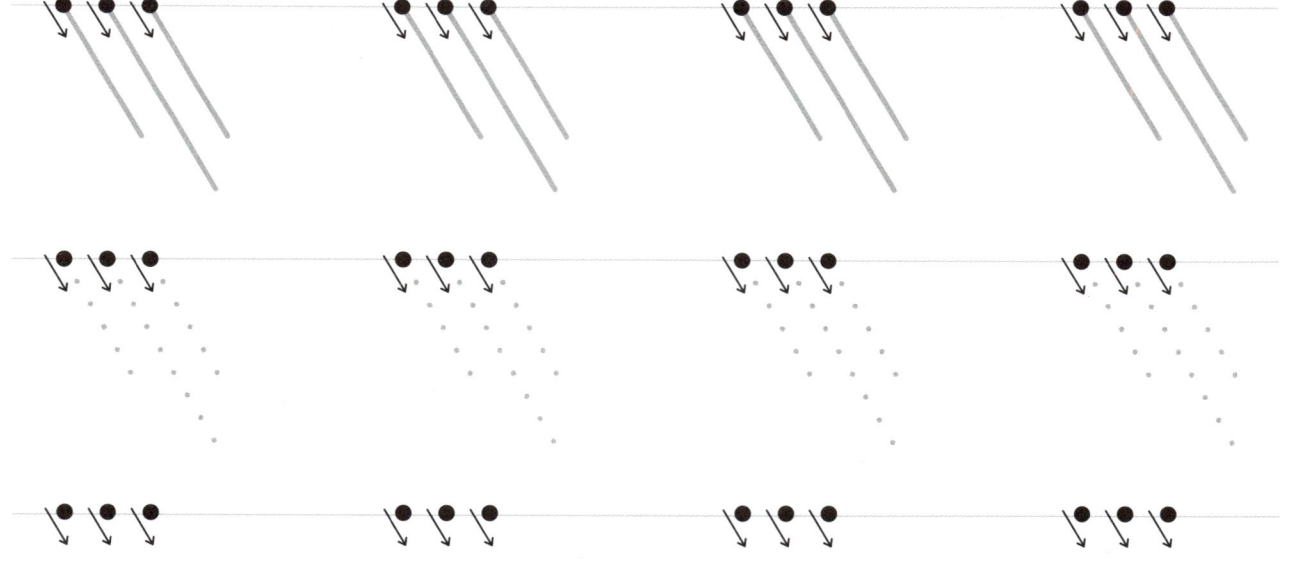

Unit 1: Practising patterns

Practice picture

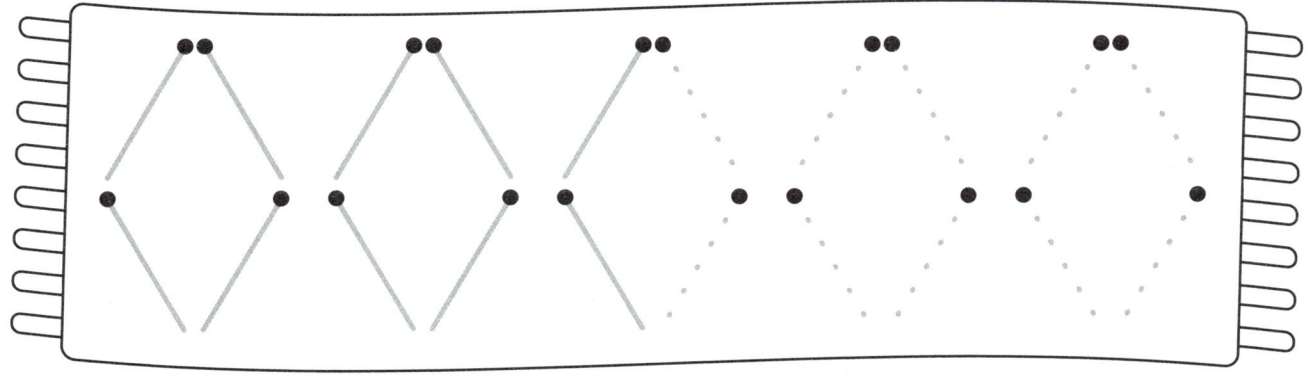

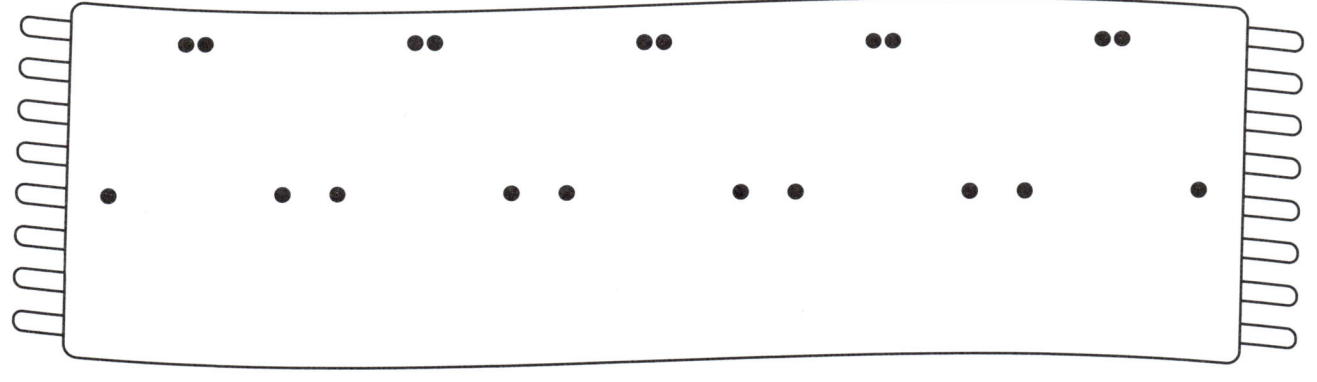

Pattern check-up

25

Unit 1: Practising patterns

Draw over and copy the zig-zags.

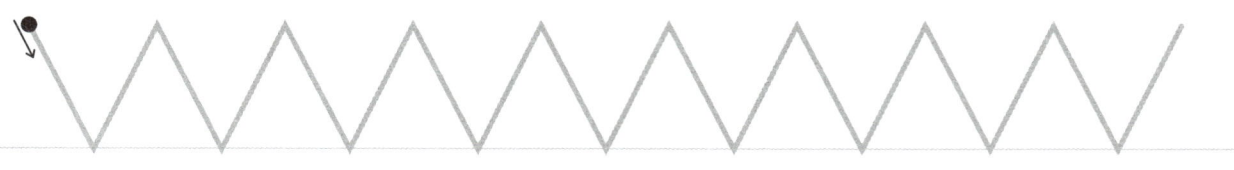

Draw over and copy the zig-zags.

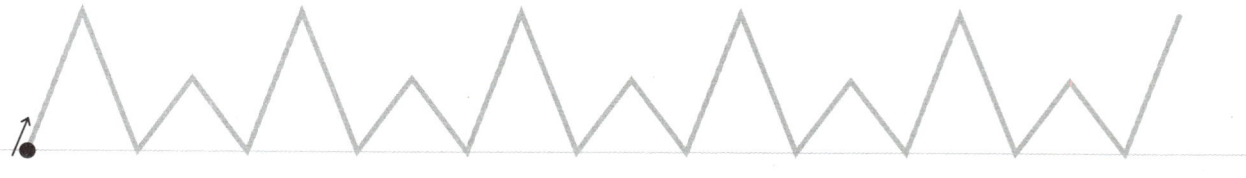

Unit 1: Practising patterns

Practice picture

Pattern check-up

Unit 1: Practising patterns

Draw over and copy the lines.

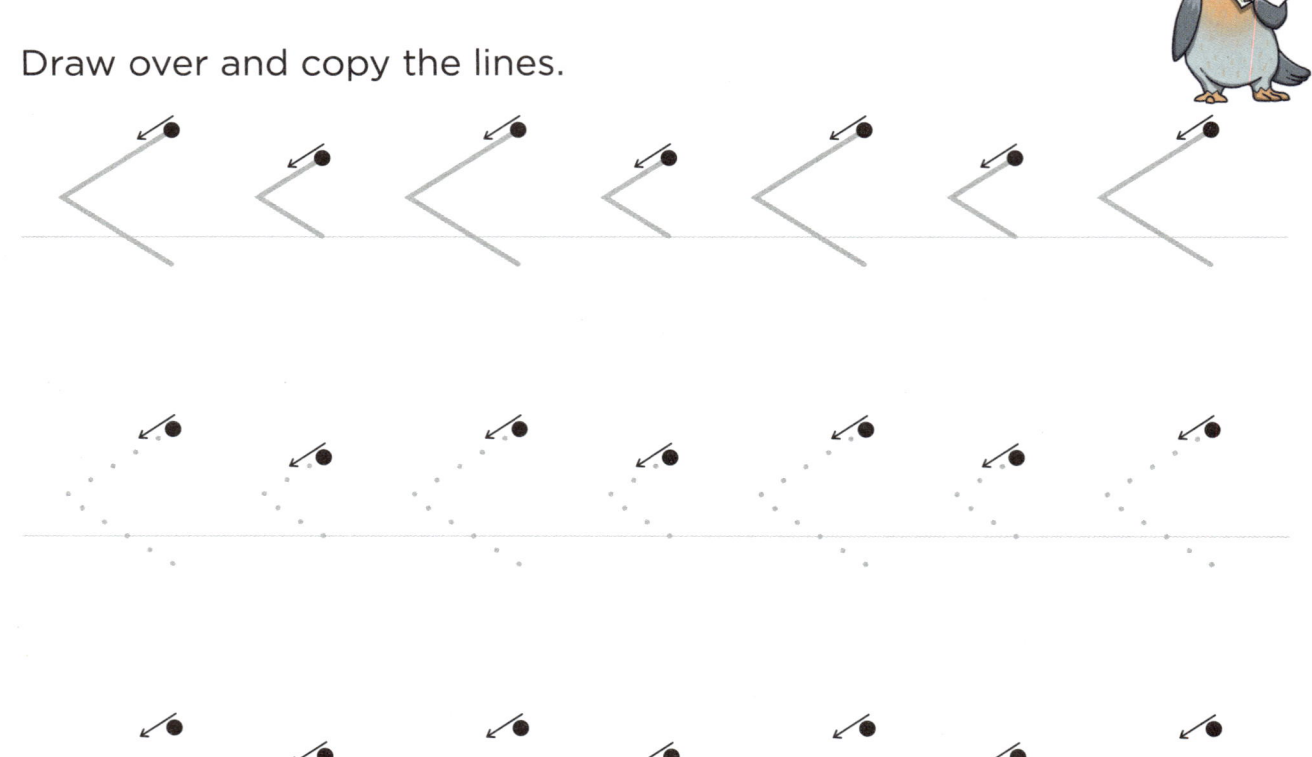

Draw over and copy the lines.

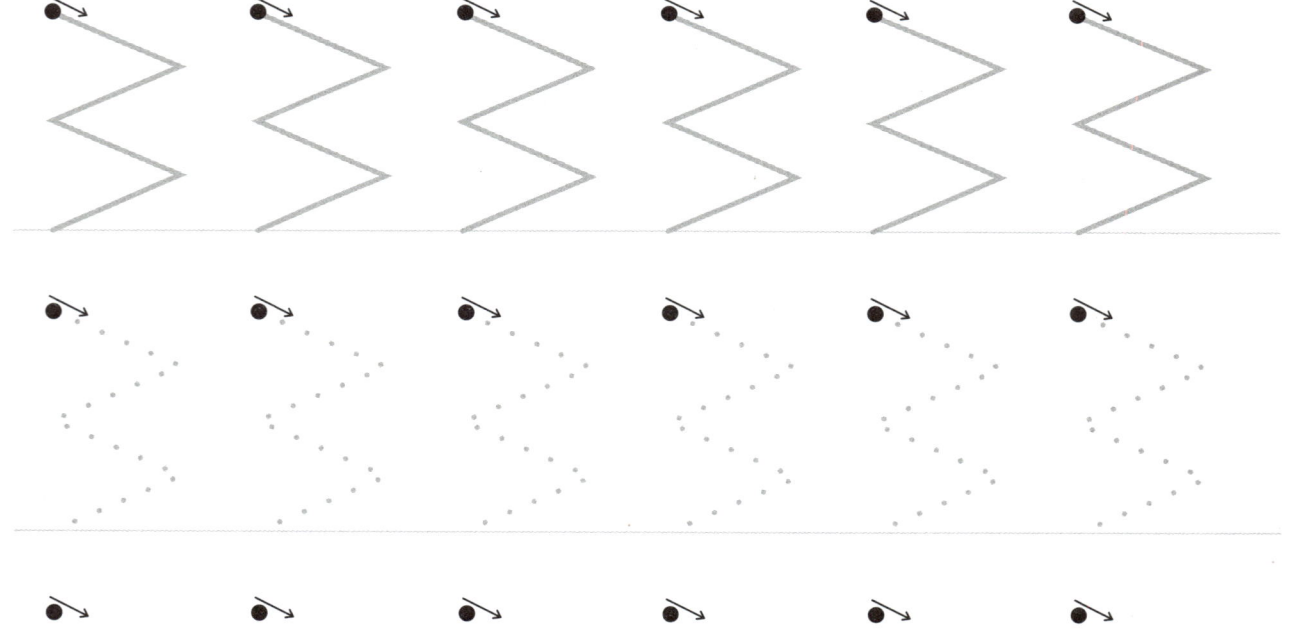

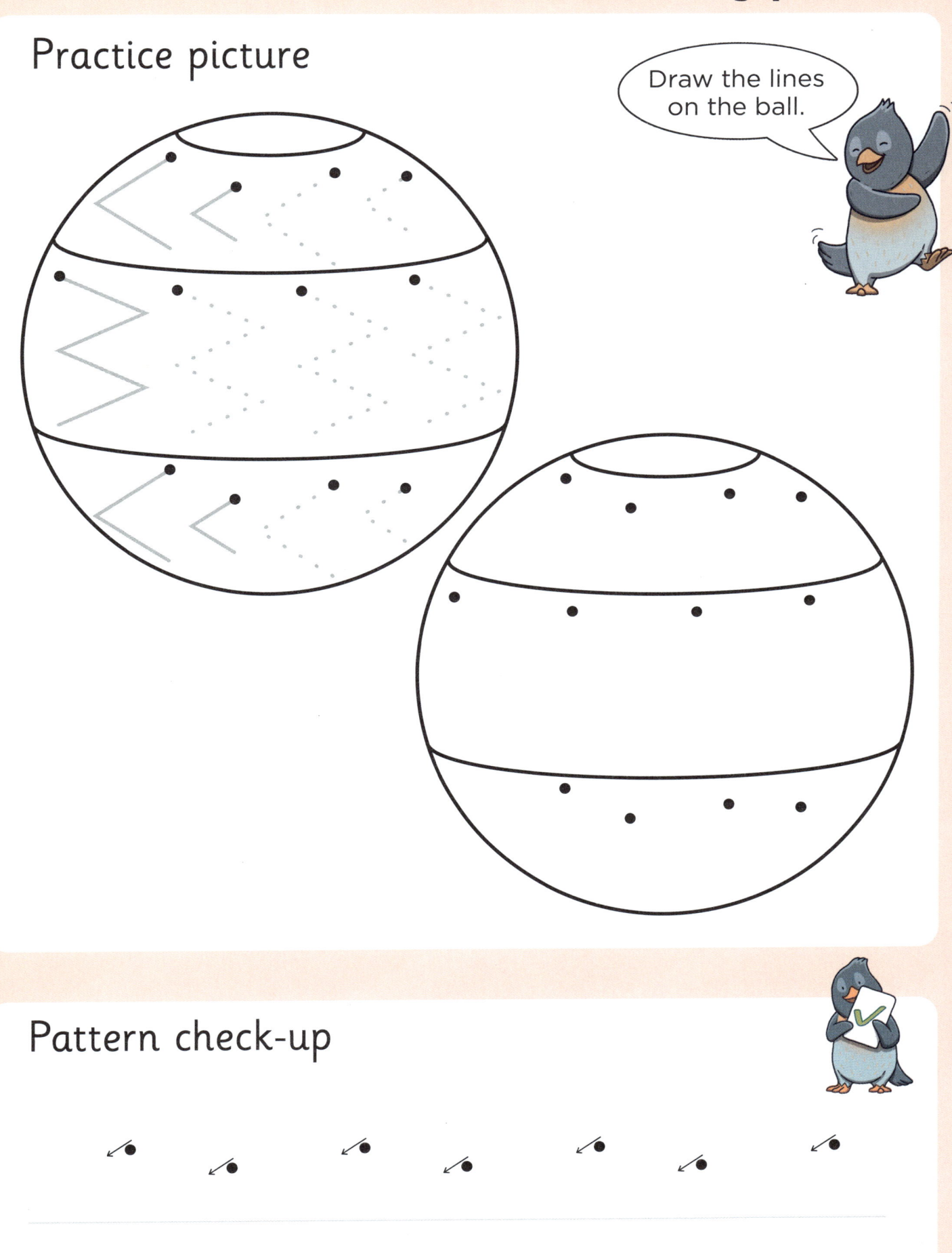

Unit 1: Practising patterns

Draw over and copy the crosses.

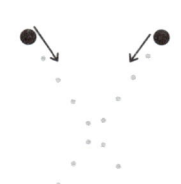 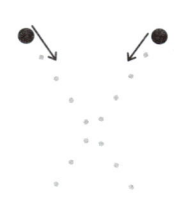  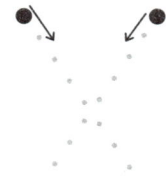 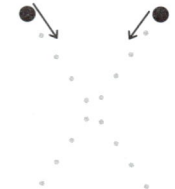

Draw over and copy the crosses.

    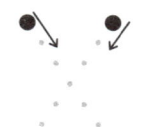

Unit 1: Practising patterns

Practice picture

Draw the crosses on the crown.

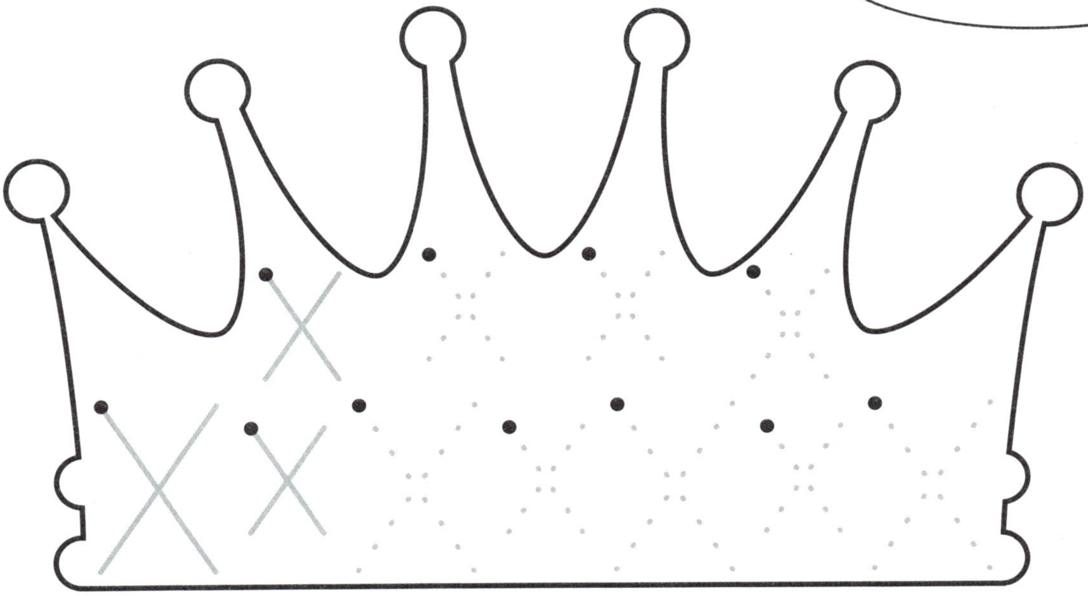

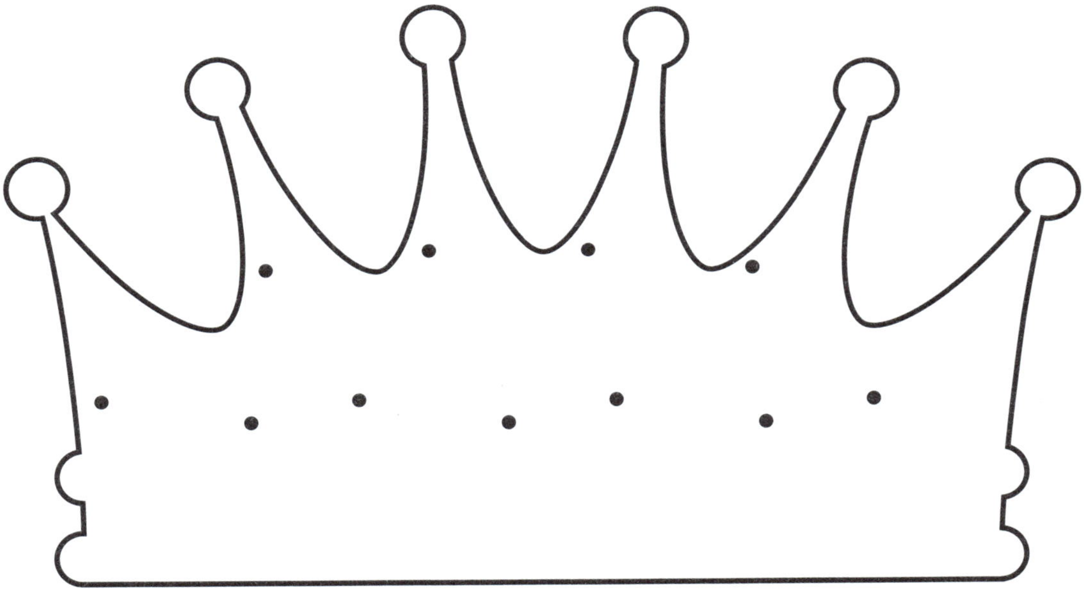

Pattern check-up

Unit 1: Practising patterns

Draw over and copy the triangles.

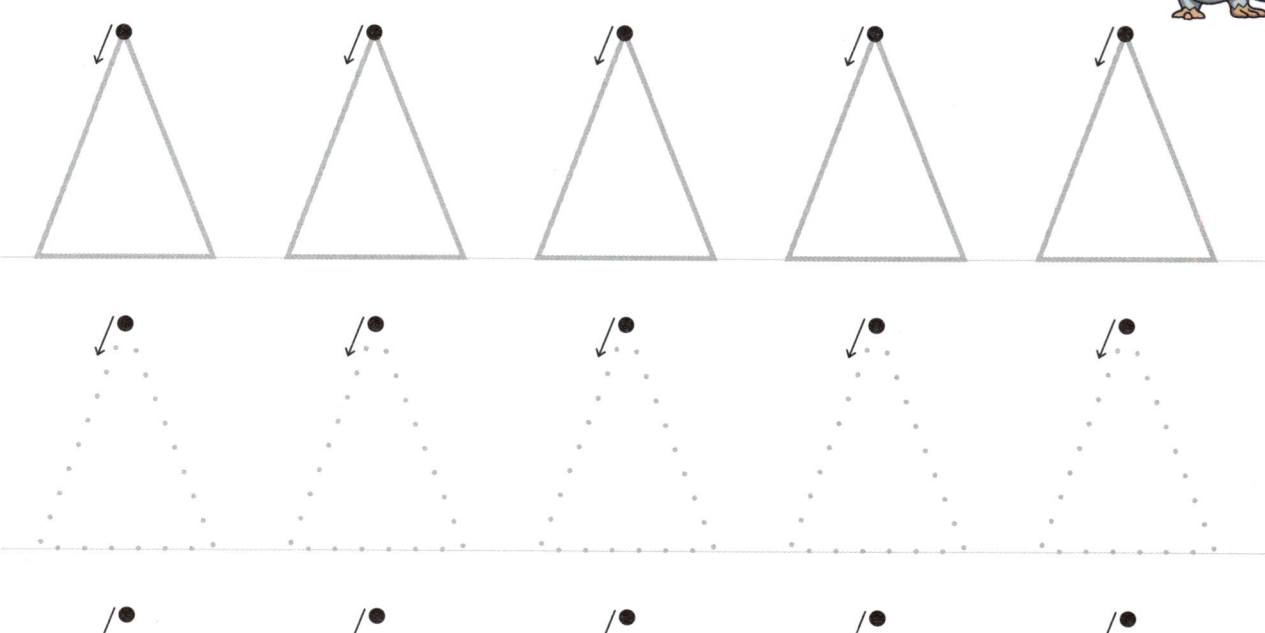

Draw over and copy the triangles.

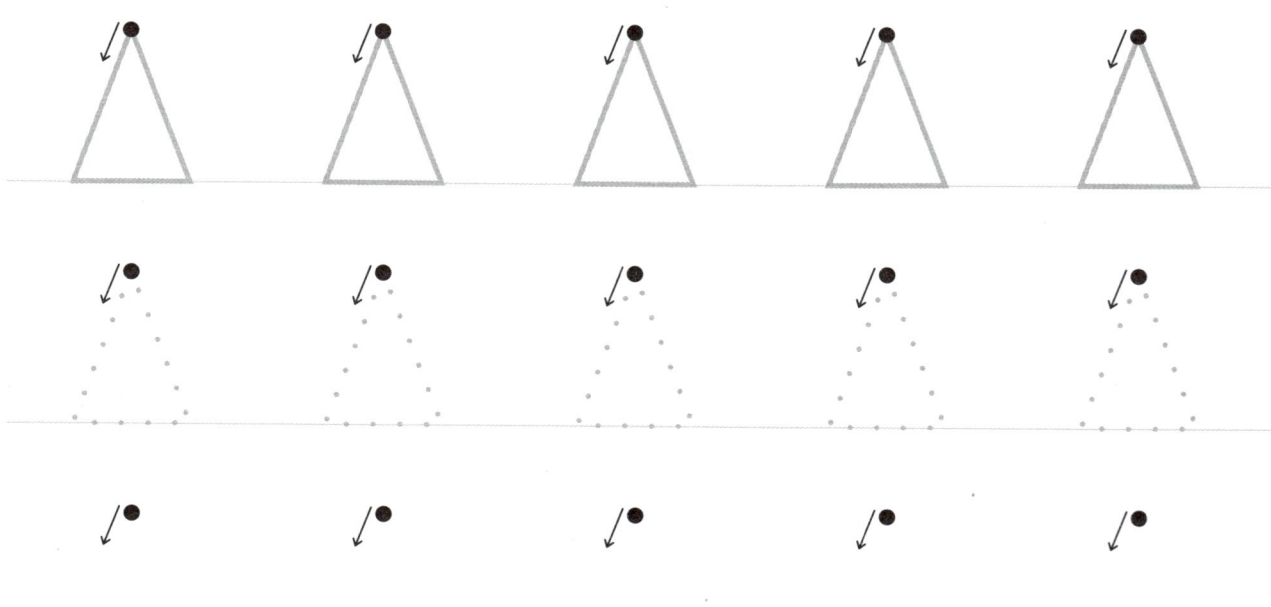

Unit 1: Practising patterns

Practice picture

Draw the tops of the trees.

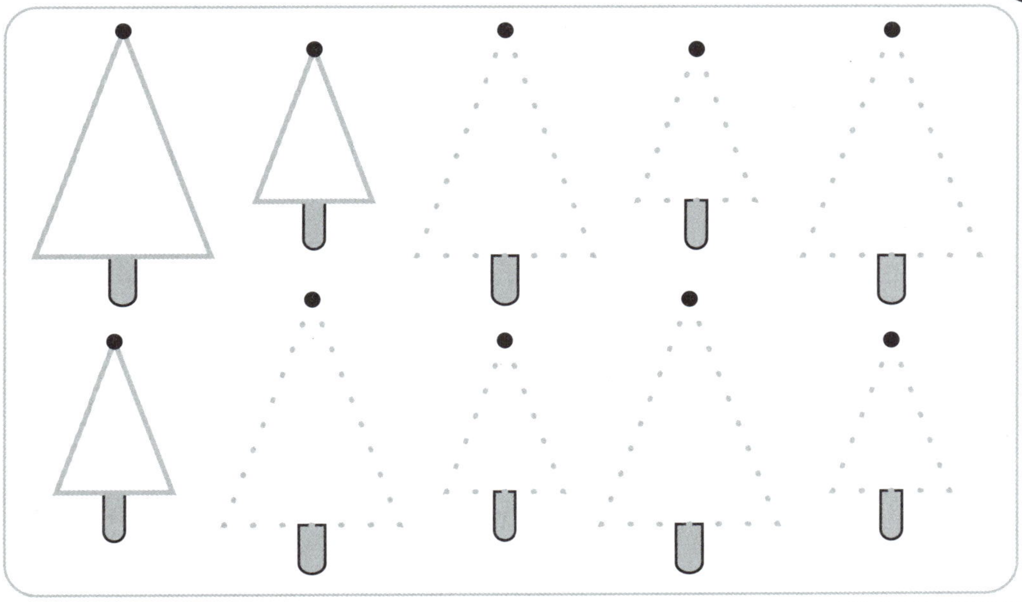

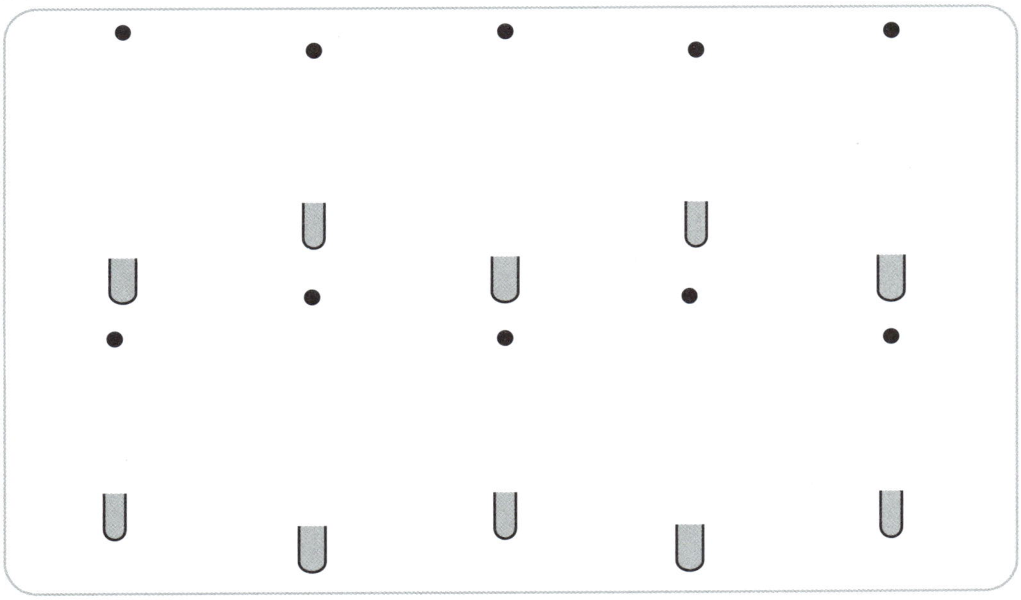

Pattern check-up

33

Practice

Practice

Practice

Practice

Practice

Practice

William Collins' dream of knowledge for all began with the publication of his first book in 1819.
A self-educated mill worker, he not only enriched millions of lives, but also founded a flourishing publishing house.
Today, staying true to this spirit, Collins books are packed with inspiration, innovation and practical expertise.
They place you at the centre of a world of possibility and give you exactly what you need to explore it.

Published by Collins
An imprint of HarperCollins*Publishers*
The News Building, 1 London Bridge Street, London, SE1 9GF, UK

HarperCollins*Publishers*
Macken House, 39/40 Mayor Street Upper, Dublin 1, D01 C9W8, Ireland

Browse the complete Collins catalogue at
collins.co.uk

Text © Rachel Davis and Manreet Ratan 2025. Text licensed exclusively to HarperCollins*Publishers* Ltd.
Design © HarperCollins*Publishers* Ltd 2025
Illustrations © Wandle Learning Trust 2025

Wandle Learning Trust name and logo © Wandle Learning Trust

Created in collaboration with Wandle Learning Trust.
www.littlewandle.org.uk

10 9 8 7 6 5 4 3 2

A catalogue record for this publication is available from the British Library.

ISBN 978-0-00-880029-1

All rights reserved. No part of this publication may be reproduced, stored in a retrieval system, or transmitted in any form by any means, electronic, mechanical, photocopying, recording or otherwise, without the prior written permission of the Publisher or a licence permitting restricted copying in the United Kingdom issued by the Copyright Licensing Agency Ltd, 5th Floor, Shackleton House, 4 Battle Bridge Lane, London SE1 2HX.

Without limiting the exclusive rights of any author, contributor or the publisher of this publication, any unauthorised use of this publication to train generative artificial intelligence (AI) technologies is expressly prohibited. HarperCollins also exercise their rights under Article 4(3) of the Digital Single Market Directive 2019/790 and expressly reserve this publication from the text and data mining exception.

Authors: Rachel Davis and Manreet Ratan
Publisher: Laura White
Product manager: Holly Woolnough
Copyeditor: Sarah Snashall
Proofreader: Sally Byford
Illustrator: Noah Warnes
Cover designer: Kneath Associates
Internal designer: David Jimenez
Typesetter: 2Hoots Publishing Services Ltd
Production controllers: Katharine Willard and
    Sophie Waeland

Wandle Learning Trust and Little Sutton Primary School have partnered with HarperCollins*Publishers* to provide teachers with a full systematic synthetic phonics programme, Little Wandle Letters and Sounds Revised, and accompanying Collins Big Cat readers. Full details of the programme, including CPD training, can be found at www.littlewandlelettersandsounds.org.uk.

Printed and bound in the UK using 100% Renewable Electricity at Martins the Printers Ltd

collins.co.uk/sustainability